THERE WILL BE NO MORE DAUGHTERS

CHRISTINE LARUSSO

&NOW Books
Lake Forest College
2019

First published 2019 by &NOW Books, an imprint of Lake Forest College Press.

Carnegie Hall
Lake Forest College
555 N. Sheridan Road
Lake Forest, IL 60045

lakeforest.edu/andnow

Lake Forest College Press publishes in the broad spaces of Chicago studies. Our imprint, &NOW Books, publishes innovative and conceptual literature and serves as the publishing arm of the &NOW writers' conference and organization.

ISBN: 978-1-941423-03-5

Book design by Jakob Vala

Printed in the United States

LAKE FOREST
COLLEGE
PRESS

BOOKS

For all the daughters

For Elizabeth Anne "Pinky" Quon (née Buchanan),
a daughter, a wife, a mother, a victim, an addict, an Angeleno,
a strong-coffee-drinker, a bowler—my grandmother

For Los Angeles

INTRODUCTION

Artists reckon with the political by engaging with the histories of our elders, particularly those unable to inscribe themselves. Poetry is a unique space for that inquiry as it draws from the wells of subjectivity and interiority to project out history inflected with the sensual life of the body. Less fact, more feeling maybe, but as Gloria Anzaldua would argue, "The body—that site which houses the intuitive, the unspoken, the viscera of our being—this is the revolutionary promise of 'theory in the flesh.'" What is a history of a community without understanding the body in that community? Bodies speak to and move around each other; we also define each other and these micro-interactions come to mirror the larger systems we move in. "I am without a map" writes Christine Larusso in *There Will Be No More Daughters*, a book that guides a reader into early-90s Los Angeles where a girl surrounded by contradicting emblems of class, race, and gender formulates a complex (and sometimes shifting) self against the newly postmodern backdrop of Los Angeles.

Larusso refracts that multiverse through an ambitious system of forms that reflect the rigor of her inquiry: instead of settling with one narrow subjective gaze, Larusso synthesizes her history in a myriad of tones and shapes. In her submission to the prize she wrote "[I] both dive into and blow apart form; to invest in the traditional as a way of cracking it open and using it as a magnifying tool to grow, advance, address and wring the historical." In the poem "Dolores," Larusso describes her grandmother's desperate struggle to survive in a place that wants to put her in a literal box while residing in the box of a bodega:

she knew the names

of the entire city of Downey

each proud citizen

in a city made entirely of factory and concrete

she wanted to know

and   uplift

Larusso evokes the dry air of Southern California but her use of the page also heightens her ironic tone as she uses (and dismantles) the language of the company line as enacted by the city's landscape shaped by the company, the factory the city. Later, in the poem-essay-poetics statement "The Letting Go," we find Larusso's affinity with film as the landscape against which she boldly plays out her interrogation of prettiness and its fascinating twin subject: alcoholism, "the many generations locked in a locket." This lacerating autobiography also critiques the damage of assimilation and Larusso puts herself right into the center of it:

> What I haven't spoken about is the mirror. Here goes. It feels like I'm plunging into deep water. I will take my clothes off, and I will see some version of myself in the mirror. I don't know anymore if it is actually what I look like or not. Things have become very blurry: there's the fat girl I see, there's the thin girl people tell me I am, there's the average sized, broad-shouldered woman I know I must be, given my measurements, my size, the way people talk about me.

This is how she understands her body is being read in the world, which she uses to decode how she makes self. The cool analysis of this gesture is thrilling. Larusso takes ownership of the discourse as a way of moving past it. She's not seeking resolution or amends or empathy. She's alongside the women in this poem and the women surrounding the poem asking the same questions forging ahead pitilessly against the same demons.

Larusso is an exciting new voice because she is rigorous and exacting and wholly original while also being extraordinarily thoughtful and compassionate towards her subject, even herself. This book is important because it is beautifully well-crafted and because it's a potent consideration of how complexly drawn we are in our histories and in our vulnerabilities.

—Carmen Giménez Smith

THERE WILL BE NO MORE DAUGHTERS

CONTENTS

BEHOLDER / 1

FALSE MEMORY SYNDROME / 5

HOURGLASS / 7

AMERICAN GIRL / 9

FORTUNE / 11

DOLORES / 12

DAUGHTER: ASYMPTOMATIC / 18

CELL DEATH / 20

EXPERIMENT TO PROVE THE EXISTENCE OF COLOR UNDERWATER / 25

I WAS A PAINTER ONCE / 26

RIGOR MORTIS / 43

DAUGHTER: MEMORIA OBSCURA / 47

EXTRACTION / 49

LUNAR UNDERSTANDING / 50

COVET / 52

GOSHOGAOKA / 53

BLISSED BY BADNESS / 56

ERASURE OF SELF AS SEATED NUDE / 58

BRINE / 61

IN ORDER TO CRACK THE EGG WHILE PRESERVING THE YOLK / 62

EXTINCTION / 63

MINIMALISM / 65

ODE TO MY LOVER'S BED / 67

CENTO OF PAST LOVERS / 68

SHAPES / 74

THE LETTING GO / 76

PURLSPRUNG / 94

THERE WILL BE NO MORE DAUGHTERS / 96

BIVALVE / 98

BEHOLDER

I was raised in the long hallway of a meat freezer,
the one place in my family's bodega where I later
learned I could hide and couldn't be found. This is Downey.
The 80s. Soon to be the 90s. The riots hitch their hands
to the back of our trucks. The riots make noise, tampons
and stacks of cash get stolen, the Whittier earthquake
roars as the liquor bottles crash to the floor. My grandmother,
born in Watts, South Los Angeles, L.A. to the *first*
gen, landscape of taco trucks and oil refineries, insisted
on feel-good American fare: the BBQs, pool swims, hot
dogs with electric-colored ketchup and mustard.
Memory is in the mind of the beholder.
There was no table to be Chinese here. There was no room
to write our quickly loosening second language, *perdido*,
perdido, perdido. We did not have a closet grand enough for lineage—
we called it *hapa*—is that why I waited this long to write
this poem? Is that why my grandfather wanted a white mistress?
I was raised on a mesa in a hot summer, a home on a road
that broke the pattern of streets named after astronauts,
space travel and satellites: a golden jewel in a post-war
world, an easter egg tucked under the persimmon tree's
rocks. I was raised to believe that beauty was better the more
pastel. Beauty was wide eyes and teeth like welcome windows.

Beauty was *no sons or daughters of mine will become*
an artist, a writer, you're better off as lawyers. The dirty
behind-the-homes hill where kids could sneak and drink beer
has been redeveloped. Tract homes like candy kisses shot out
from the machine. The split-level basement grill is now
a hot tub. When I took my father's name, I hoped to avoid
confusion. I can't go a week without being asked what I am,
hapa, mixed plate, chicana, mainland, multi, multi, multi,
I contain multitudes. How strange to find yourself in your home
again, with a tradition invented by televisions and microwave
dinners. Memory is in the mind of the beholder. How strange
to open the red envelope and see play-doh, apple pie, honeysuckle,
Christmas carols. I was raised not knowing my Chinese name,
nor my Mexican one, nor the word to describe my body
seeking the signal and syntax to guide my path through the woods.

FALSE MEMORY SYNDROME

One drop cures you. Two
faints you weak. In the   eventide picture show,
                                          the crowd stands to see
                                 you stand.

                                          The actors placed their curse.
                 Lines on the wall.

                                          Buggy and red. The sweat.
                          The heat tied round your waist.

Lifting glass lids, you faeriebook thin and ripeness all

                   over. All over a newness and these skinny
          fingers. Over and over a
                          newness.

                 Memory serum, dissolver, revolver in liquid form.

                 You doebreath
                                          and slumber. Packets of anise
          to halfwake
                          you in your sleep.

Topped off   a bit of storyoak and aching weald. A horrible,
                    salt-dissolving whisper.
                                        Wanting

                                            and with heavy shoes,
                            we ask you to keep running.

HOURGLASS

Many months would pass but no one would call this girl
a hero for sitting in the back of the Hyundai letting another

teenage girl pluck the beauty of tweendom away I was
the one being plucked and I was on the verge of

a breakdown my body so hot with hormones, my hypo-
thalamus cooking a feast, *I think I am going to pass out*

I said as my hips slid down the car seat widening getting
ready for wanting saying No saying Yes of searching

for my parents at the time still so alive but so soon
not, a spirit-fog hovering over the rim of my glasses

I searched; the hourglass emptied, the black hair
on my legs growing like Redwoods I want to keep it

as the ephemeris of this year, this day, glowing as only
hallucinogens make you glow, in spite of the locks on

every doorknob I am not a hero, merely candy-handed
all my flim-flam making music for fandangos and waltzes

I trace the highway maps on my Rand McNally scribbled
on my wrist with a sharpie the way to boys' homes I break

friendships in half dream of tattoos the Hyundai is getting

warmer it's not even sunny today in L.A. for once I went years

and years without water I was too frightened by my own body

AMERICAN GIRL

My grandmother bought me a doll   she said
                    she cost   so much   it had
       blue eyes   and   blonde braids   *I couldn't afford*
accessories   she housed the doll   in a spare room
                    it was my room at the time   we
       were on   the way   to the bowling   alley
                              my grandmother had

       arthritis   collected tiny spoons   from   cruises
    the doll   perched   like a passerine or   a thrush
a little plastic stand   to mount it upright
          so it stared or   glared   into my   eyes
              I couldn't sleep   *don't you think she's pretty*
my grandmother   asked   I had no idea
              what beauty   could be

       did think I knew   the not: not hair   dark like oil
          flat feet   not wide hips despite my age
                    fingers too
crooked   for piano-playing (I failed that lesson again and again)
    not eyes   the color of a nut tree   not this
spare room   who could ever   feel
       truly alone in this room, a flower needs light to bloom

the doll   sat dangerously   close   to the mirror
      I saw more   than one   at least doubles,   two braids,
two eyes   my grandmother
                    did not have dolls   as a child
and I suspect   no one ever   called her pretty
we gave the doll a name   something to say goodnight to
          a Callie or Emma or   white

a white name to seize   my fingers banged   at the piano
      looking   to be good at   anything   the doll was
great at being tall   for a doll   my grandmother
          would get upset if I did not brush her   blonde braids
even when
                    I was unkempt   a minor wreck, major key

she finally bought the accessories   won a bowling
          game   or two felt there was   pocket money
for Callie or Emma or [   ]   to have
      a little knapsack of books   kept in plastic   fake leather satchel
dangling   off her small   doll hips   sleeping
   with emptiness as the pages   were blank   and blank
          emptiness is no way to fill dreams   I would hear
      my grandmother's insomnia   the house creaked
                    singing old songs in a language I would never learn to speak

10

FORTUNE

All hands were set to task:
at Christmas, we unwrapped

the golden egg, lifted its
aureate skin to reveal a single

key, which swayed right and
left, denoting the two doors

it was meant to open. The
light released rainbows

in the corner of the room.
Turn the key right, unlock

a cerise '58 Corvette, meant
for a white woman (not

pictured). My grandmother
held the frame of the second

door shut, as she watched
from the stairtop, a red-tail hawk.

DOLORES

I see my grandmother

growing up in Watts

she would be subjected to the

torture of *the box,*   I see her

with the sparrow hair my grandmother   did not comb,

I see

owl-eye 80s glasses she squints through. I hear

language, a Jackson Pollock-painting of Spanish/of English/of
  Los Angeles-isms and

I see

the States

my grandmother wanted, believed in,

the histories she shed in order to be *American, North American,*

I see all her loss in Dolores, who I have never seen.

Dolores

in solitary confinement, Dolores
          after solitary confinement, trying to navigate

      Anaheim but always   getting lost,

   each street a new street an old street

    who can remember when the walls were the same for so long?

      My grandmother worked the cash register
          of my grandfather's   bodega

     her fingers

smelled like one-dollar bills   she knew the names
          of the entire city of Downey
          each proud citizen

   in a city made entirely of factory and concrete

she wanted to know

        and   uplift

she believed in this, *Chicana*

        she believed she could be uplifted. To what?

"The brain is comprised of 100 billion cells, 500 trillion connections,"
a neuroscientist reports. "It is an organ of social function.
The brain needs to interact in the world."

The neuroscientist would say my grandmother was *stimulated by a
community*.

        Dolores, I wish you were not—
        I can barely finish—
        I am ashamed—

the stress of being alone can cause the brain
to malfunction, release hormones that
affect the hippocampus, which narrows our view
of the world forever.

The boxes are 6 x 9 feet.
Usually have no windows.
The inmates must stay in the boxes
for over 20 hours a day. Usually 22.
Sometimes 23.

In order to test

    the effects

        of the box on mice, one must receive

            special permission from animal care orgs.

    There is no special permission granted to humans.

                My grandmother

sits in the back room of the bodega,
writing checks, counting checks,
signing her name the same

        opened
            a checking account
       roasted
            beef for dinners

            knew the birthdays
            of everyone on her street.

Graduate students sat alone
in small chambers, being studied.
They dropped out due to hallucinations.

I talk to myself again.
I see stars on the concrete floor,

        searching for an attic in the big
           house my grandmother
           raised her children in finding

        Easter

       eggs she hid on the roof.
         Doing the drugs
         the teenagers did in her backyard.

"The neurons stop connecting."

       It occurs to me that I am *American.*

        What would she

               say, what would either
of these women who I—am I—*hallucinating* are one woman

what would they say?

  If it wasn't on an old Western or pinned to the bulletin
board in the back office it's possible she would say nothing.

  Luxury, check-writing, histories to burn and burn and burn.

This shame is a small thing I can swallow,
  something to keep private in the morning.
I want a pill, a small and silver pill. A slow dissolve to make it go away.
  The histories won't stop calling from the grave.

DAUGHTER: ASYMPTOMATIC

Not the either/or you mistook me for I painted
    the curve of the glacier with the arch of my foot, curiouser
        and curiouser to know how much sadness I would witch upon

your wedding day. It took years for me to be
    anti-matrimony, anti-vow, anti-self-less-and-self-lost. My
        town washes itself away, ocean current, tsunami, high-winded

and heat stroke. Depression is an ice floe
    coming at your boat. That which breaks me. I feel colder as
        I grow older, less in love but instead carrying fear like a knapsack

too heavy for my back. The birds fly into my
    window and die. They lose direction, the winds keep shifting.
        There's no south left. Two pink pills help me find the dreamscape,

the verdant, the field that could keep giving
    and giving. A field of love, of birth, of life. I am without a map.
        I need no fire, no reassurance. But then, the dream takes its own turn,

as dreams do, pulls a nightshade from the
  nightmare's well. I grab the dead birds from my pockets, their fat
    bodies without air. I plant them. I bless them, the only human left. What

    was green is now ash. What was love is now grief.

CELL DEATH

Voices can wisp and still pierce;
I've felt it. At twenty. I remember
a stop light. I grew crutch-heavy,
felt-lined on the outtake—there
were many more walls, all shouldering.

The hazy windowpane.

Things that remind me of my father
include: talk radio, the Sports section,
Sinatra. An eagle I spotted in Canada.

A kitten laid down in new snow.
Radio comes from the word *radiate*
—invasion of space. A tool nature
uses to fool us, render some nights
slumberless. My bed is a mash of
fabrics and licked-away wishes.
When I was two, I wanted
nothing more than a make-believe
kitchen set. The same year I jerked
an iron from its perch, burnt a triangle
into my hip. It's still there, if you care.

Transmission: my father taught me
to twirl pasta into a spoon. Transmission:
my mother tells a story of riding
in a friend's Jeep down the Pacific Coast
Highway, being stopped by the cops,
later the friend explained why he sweated
so much: the ten or more pounds of cocaine
in the truck. Before, I was embarrassed
of this history. Now I think: what luck.
To get away.
I see tunnels of intellect that divided
my father and my mother as geomagnets.
Cells that once pushed forward weakened
ten times faster than scientists expected.
Transmission: I have written many words
around static to try and silence it.
I have thorns of memories that are not mine:
rosebuds growing in my limbic system,
a mountain slope in perpetual bloom.
Pluck one rose: a man holds a knife
to my mother's throat. He is a father.
He is somebody's father. Who belongs to him?

Who do I belong to?

For as many sunsets. For the clocks I lost
count. As I called myself an orphan before
I was one. I did check statistics, facts,
information: *the most obvious symptoms
are movement-related; these include shaking,*
rigidity, slowness of movement and difficulty
with walking and gait

and

idiopathic (having no known cause)

I walk briskly. Even in humidity.

I hold my hand above my head in side-
angle pose. My spine. I think about
my own decline often, tell jokes about
my demise happening before I turn 40.

Transmission: my father's entire livelihood,
income depended on the strength of his
body and his confidence that it would not
betray him. I call what happened *beguilement.*
This is an understatement. *Parkinson's primary*
feature is cognitive decline, which can lead to hallucination.

I pull What Ifs from a pillow, (the spot
I once fished for dollars and luck) pinch
the base of my neck, *hippocampus, limbic
system, cerebral cortex.* As drawn to the brain
as I am afraid. Where memory is stored—
the death of dopamine-producing neurons—
Where memory is destroyed. Destroys?

What do knives remind you of?

A shaking woman. She's not cold,
it's California. There's something else:
a prismatic hour feasting on the room.
I watch a man torched from a photograph.
A smoking car. It seems like all the women
are running away, have been running, never
stopping. Was it her father? My own? Genetic,
ancestral. Hereditary, patrimonial.

To err is human, to persist is devilish.

This is not my tale to invoke and warm
by the stove. *Old shoe, black shoe. Died
before I had time.* Counting my steps, I'm
a tick-tock at a quick clip. Car-want. Car-thirst.
Car-hunger and hanker.
An orphan must learn to love the highway.
I see a three-year-old palm in the hand
of another (a kind of astrology, divination).
The hours before I taught myself lessons
of on-ramps, geography, tectonics.

Transmission: in this telling, no drought.
In this telling, I have yet to move
through the space of a quake, the vicious,
headstrong earth. I ask the man (is it
my father?), *What wet?* And he says, *This
is rain. Rain. How could you forget?*

EXPERIMENT TO PROVE THE EXISTENCE OF COLOR UNDERWATER

All scab and seawrack but this was a lake—no familiar escape—I was chuffed in a blue coat bottle—body a hollow—body mnemonic—locate the stare: of the eyes: of the man: stare back—no escape—body a lake—an azure revision—I learned to swim by sinew—wreck-taught—a scrabble I mastered to skim—body sour and saline—body a wave—I erased page after page—the lake, the chapter—I pasted the man: with this glue: with this hand: *this* hand: onto the page—his body my body all paste—am I unframed, unmasked, uncouth?—body crossed out, an *x*—a spectrum—if I were celestial, if able to wash out the beryl—if I chose to be bawdy, a fullblown mystery—if I was woolslept, gloomed to a T—fraught without floret, later lost to the frost—body a bulb—I swim to write this but the ink will not stick—how he—body an eraser—an answer—*the white is nothing if not for the black—the white is nothing if not for the black*—the body a story without ending—the body the lake—two bodies—seasoned, a soiled beige—body a curfew and brine—and if I were wicked enough to tame a tide, I would—it was an experiment, a definition—liquid poured into a vessel, a boat, the emptying of an egg—body viscous—I aimed to remove the ash and pallid—pinched the tool between my fore and thumb—I was brash, this once, this erase—corked at either end—body defined, finally lineated— was there time?—what was in the crimson, I wondered? A must of me—the skin on the surface—I swear by the inversion, the unique—as I was saying, as I was swimming, *a spectrum, a spectrum*—

I WAS A PAINTER ONCE

a shed for mangled   gouache,

         landscape miscalculated,

   I was a canvas

discarded, sighed into, sight of life I say to you:

it is unfair to blame the car. The girl who drove the car.
         Her tightwhip steel curls. Turns.
    Any curved distraction

          steel poured over

  linen

and me   my   oh   my

                                      hard to say

                                            name—

this now nameless painter

                        admits:

                  I cast my clothes

            for the specks and the drops.

                  Of course it was the yellow that
            killed. The dense lines
left you   near an edge

            in the crease of the ocean's hollow hand,

seawashed starfish underwished upon

waveless—blameless—

The news of Andrew's death, a fog at my door, looting the light
  that tried to pass into me.

*

Once I woke, my migraine gnashing—

I knew—

The mauve flesh of my palm that did not hold

onto you

tight enough.

I was a painter once,
did stab and slash and chew.   I wished you upon it and
  then off it again.

I wished for my throat
to violinstring and there

to be no   slab for
water
to run

or rescue. I wished

for a cliff.

I was

the paint too

—sticky—

a sealant nailing
hummingbirds to the revolving

door of your   mouth.

This grief dries up and sticks with one brush
like the shed's torso and tenement,
fixes the solid, the matter we stand on and with one stroke,

invokes cicadas, winds of madness,

color inverted:

this is grief, this is her

*

I was painful once.   I used lush darkness to lure you

And I could only be hushed white when you were

glassy open window and no breeze

stripped away little river
be careful be careful not to paint the ravine   too thin
                                                                    too

alone   without

rocks

*

I was the tool too,
the slab of metal dragging chemically tight colors across
tarp
and later,
the bombhot thigh
that held steel close,
a wired, bright
sex shining its touch,

graphite ignited—

*

I was a waiting room,

a broken clock, running on a generator of desire

the final
plunk

little phoenix, lonely bird, a hitchhiker for oxygen,

failing

total
emulsion

*

I was,
    I was,
        I was varnished

I sprawled to save

the corner of Sunset where your mother penciled
irises on a brick wall where they found the teacup
                temporal—cerebellum—occipital
                less bloody

                identifiable

                                        shards of
        canine, molar, humerus

                                radius

                                scapula
                                        sternum

                                        ulna
                                                bones
                        I never thought

                                        I'd know this close

                                *

                        iris iris,
        there were irises I caught myself

                deep   enameled

                                sleepcity

*

I was depowered   a hue in ashwater   halfalive and afloat in the sink

I hugged the glass walls of the library

I did   I did exactly   what you told me not
                                                            to

took the Sexton out of the brick wall
          thumbed dictionary thin pages the anthology

trying to   become a building thinking I could
                              harden myself   become a shield
                    against
          the goings/on   the wrack and shatter

          it is June   *I am tired of being brave*

took Sexton and licked a page edged in grief framed

in gold leaf

where you scribbled,   to me

There's nothing worse   than feeling bad and not   being able to tell

you.

It's space. It's space. It's space.

*

I was
       a painter

no mere

jupiter

crayon,

jupiter

transmitter

who

left

auspices

undressed

at home

mistook what I could mean to you—

I was used to being alone.

Was always one in

    a vulnerable cave, moonlight-guide, moonlight-afraid,

        moonlight-love—and there, alone,

            I asked the night to darken itself

            *

        You were

            suspended

          and saturate-eyed

                      shortsight

         Of course the California Incline and

                descent. Of course the
             phone not clicking

                                          to warn

streets   concrete

                how landslide looms

                sea unloosed

                        *

I was not the boat   and neither, not ever   were you.

        In fact, I forgot   about the boat.

I was not the boat but I was some object for mechanical leverage and later:
    failure. I was held in your mother's hands as
        we both overlooked   the horizon, ombre of nature's indifference.
                I was cleaned
                            bleached, germ-free, the wrong fit.
    The wrong size. Your mother held me in her hands.
Your mother held me   and the noise between her ears
    the noise and fuzz the *fuck this*   *fuck this place*   Your mother
considering the depth of the ocean, the stretch of H2O   the plastic
    island the width of Texas   the necessity of the highway
                the travertine—the steel—the concrete
        the halo of emission circling above the city   it is a restless,
    uneasy, place   *this could have happened to anyone*   your
mother with the fuzz between
        her ears   me germ-free
            finding it hard to paint in all this water

I was not the boat.

*

You need to write about the pebble of guilt. I pinpricked this note into my

thigh. I remember walking into the Pacific—

there was no bottom

I remember walking I did not feel

a damn thing but one

one pebble. I would walk into the school auditorium two weeks later,

the faces of my classmates wide and all sixteen years old
so many full moons in that shiny room

skin waxy as the floor

You need to talk about this one would whisper to me

another would just stare and I would dig my nails into my thighs.
Searching for the pebble of guilt I sewed inside.
Trying to paint the 3D but it's
all

slack and straight,

the cloth of this mind.
All seams releasing at the same time—

*

*

You can't invent landscape

*

all that goes up

sent me ballooning, inhaled and

heliumlung

this piece you

won of me,

cutup
keepsake

I was a painter,

clasped and hooked   held firm the wall

RIGOR MORTIS

You will learn about the laughter—
        the awkward, jilted escape from
                the altar of emotion—
that you will see the puddle
        of formaldehyde on the steel
                table, then laugh.
You do not know what it is
        to be seventeen but somehow,
                you are. You are
a plank of wood floating down
        a river. You cannot recall the
                names of every
naked body you have met, but
        you could count them on one
                hand. Your father
is not dead, not yet, but soon.
        You will enter the Human
                Dissection Lab
with kitten curiosity, your
        fingers running the circle
                of every jarred
tumor. You will not faint
        or fever. You will watch
                the technician

pat the garbage bag that
          covers the dead woman's
                    vagina as if
he were patting a newborn
          rabbit and you will be very
                    aware of every
hair on your arm. You are not
          the pacemaker that blinked
                    slowly off and
killed her. You did not kill
          the teenage boy, either.
                    Later you will
be a nylon, hashed and plastered
          on the wound you have from
                    running then falling
then skidding your legs on
          the driveway. You are a gash
                    brimming with
tar. You will be the sound
          of ripping the nylon away
                    from your own
once-unblemished flesh.
          Later your larynx will dust
                    like a ghosttown—
the technician will suggest
          you are allergic to the peas
                    inside the packed
lunch. You are not, will never,
          be allergic to peas. You will
                    thumb a Xanax

in your pocket, steal a scalpel
       off an unattended shelf, slice
           the pill into two
little canoes, later swallow
       the boats while sitting inside
           your parked
car, a waterfall of rubbing
       alcohol on your patella, your
           femur. You
are the unmapped abyss of the sea.
       The technician will offer you
           the dead boy's
brain to hold, and you will cup it,
       bite your lip, try not to think
           of raw meat but
it feels like raw meat. Later you
       will learn to expect the ghosts,
           the way one
expects the mailman, the exact
       time he slips invoices and
           mailorder
catalogs into the slot of the door
       of your home. You will
           know the cue
and you will climb out of your
       window. You will be locked
           by a pale
blush, by this pulse. You will
       find that every hallway
           of every

city has a cold spot, every wall
        has a chafe where the paint
                slacks and thins.

DAUGHTER: MEMORIA OBSCURA

Who said we could save
the horses? That the water

would not continue to rise,
lap at the spot our ankles

dip in? Who was the night's
liar, claiming that the children

you loved in those years
when you, too, were a child,

would not die? Who made
statements from soapboxes

about the nuclear
family, about the dinner

table always being set, about
boys? Who brought hooves

to the flame so they nearly
sparked up, said a prayer for

the homeland? Who twisted
the knob on the radio so hard

no one would believe the truth
you later cried from the roofs,

how everyone was dead or dying,
beside them a matchstick smoking

low off the ash of innocence?
The barn is on fire. The barn is on fire.

Who is left to save?

EXTRACTION

You were right
about the boat.   I could only

gather   so many
porcelain shards.

The fixture
wouldn't budge. All light
        fought against   its own

candescence.
All sonars were foiled   and hot,
                anyway.

You can tell them you let me go.

You can say
there were only
        so many bones.

LUNAR UNDERSTANDING

I have my eye on you,
Lune. I am used to pert

syrup, your saccharine for
lyricists,

the sew-handed. My taste-

buds lick alert.

My stretch marks,
a kind of trade mark.

A tree making rings.

It's hot, it's summer,—I like
        myself better

in a sweater.
And you, Lune—the name

no one
called you. They said Moon,

Moon—cooling
        the prow of a ship,
you can't give yourself a sobri-

quet. My arms at mast.

Due north, nonny nonny,
stitch your sail a name

a nod, a bottle,
and hunker for a storm.

COVET

Nowhere a billboard proclaiming I'm lonely,
but I am lonely. Finally a traffic light. Let
the mind turn green for all the mistresses and
their cloudy afternoon drinks. The angle of
your elbow & close shatter for my nasty
displeasure & want. I am neuron & neurotic.
Music looming. Wintered distress & all I can
think about is fucking. I planked tall the perfect
house but liked you small so I shrunk it, love
made miniature. Thirtyseven versions of you
for my curio cabinet, my skilled fingers kneady,
knotty. Born without an arrow. An object
without an alarm suddenly taking flight.
Finding a stone in my shirtdress warm with
an itch for you, six years too late. I am a nightslip
of naughts, not brave enough, sheer enough,
wrinkled even after having been pressed.

GOSHOGAOKA

". . . just the girls and their routines . . ."

—Tim Martin for the Museum of Modern Art

They said:

"keep writing

about the body. Also that   "the ones who keep writing will
always write." Like: the scab that heals, but: scar tissue.

Your heart may be a little candlewax.
Your heart may smoke of palo santo.

Solving for the mission, I pull each paper
from the fortune teller's desk.

You may ache on the left side.

It is Tuesday so you seek a new fate
for your spine.

Balance the datebook on your head for maximal alignment.

During the days with crystal-and-glitz
in-check, I was a locked box
with a clock inside.   I timed every move of my bone,
down to the finish line.

Play with girls but be as strong as boys.
You may ache on the left side.
When I
was young,
I didn't smile

for photographs.   When they ask why
she doesn't smile

for photographs   the tennis player says:

"I don't want to be here"

When I was a camera, I didn't smile for photographs.

Ask the code and ye shall be a locked box
with a clock inside.
Your heart may play with girls but be
as strong as boys.

They said:

"You can't be good at ballet."

With thighs like that.

Someone took a photograph
of my scar tissue   for the performance.   One man yells out.

Then another.
And another.

In a city full of men, I ask my women to build

the mountains and attack from the Forest. With thighs like that,

we can climb.

They said:

"Fish and shoot like a girl."

I have known two guns in my life
        and I know them as biceps.

I wander this forest, a key hung from my hip.
With thighs like this.

With this muscle, a compass.

BLISSED BY BADNESS

I steep tea in absinthe, watch
the fog roll off. When
I was young, I was taught to
buy stock in the tree canopies,
to bet on callow dirt as it
turned over, and over, and
over, mineraled with breath
of a new century. The ghost
of John Muir still roughs my
sleep, wakens me after
eleven. To doze, I learn
to ferment any number
of woodland gifts.
The tonics make
headlights magnify
as fireflies. As the city
builds concrete to hold stone,
the bricks pave the road to
an ocean. I was told there
were temples in the forest,
and in my own fear of
salvation, booked wheels for
a metropolis. Here: count fern

leaves, turning to burnt paper.
Here: confuse a cuckoo clock
for a goldeneye, a ruddy, or
redhead. And while we're on
the subject of species, let's
be frank: my toes are willing
to dip in a variety of muds.
The body is both the closed doors
of the church and the egret's wings.

ERASURE OF SELF AS SEATED NUDE

I want you to lick
the dirt   of all the past
Hes off of me, off   the backs of my
thighs and   ridges
of my spine.   What if
I was only

a window?
Each green
of my cell   was   open,   woodbuilt,
willing?

Each instant   you   ate the knit and wire
of my lips   you could
see,   without squinting,
the inkstreaks and
pockmarks   that fizzle
when I mumble.

                                    And what if
                        I finally   let you
                    erase me? Gave
blur and fuzz to each   fine line and grew
                                    used to you, to touch
            after   I had shuttered,

                tinted: my mouth an aperture
                                without hinge.

    I am crushpoor but need to augur you—

my only disclaimer: the swell under my clavicle means when you bite me,

                I'll bite back. The clocks and

                Orion inside our chests.

Our bodies as a room without perspective.

            My lust
                works like the tides pulling in reverse,

                    controlled
          by a simple ballast and dent.
        Controlled by
                    a solo bulb, flashlight
of the wild, the It, the master image,   crudely underlined.

          And the cave of what
                    I want—

BRINE

I long to tongue a vulgar thing, a morsel sweet. We have been here
so long, out on these dinghies, barely brigs or yawls. This wind like
betrayal, sent us looking. I keep asking the water to explain itself, but it
only reflects my bad deeds. We couldn't squall our way back to town if
we tried—air so iodine no smell of salted fish could lead us. Agnes and
me, and in the distance, an abandoned ketch, mirage of Alaskan sea,
slouching towards a reckless chasm. Agnes the first girl I wanted to kiss,
her lips cold as a coma. Her skin, livid; hair, a violent red stirring. The
mice, how Agnes drowned those mice. I can't forget it. We were only
nine years old. She ripped the whiskers out with tweezers. I thought I
would go blind after that. This I confess, but it's not my stone to carry
and I haven't the muzzle for throwing. With every anchor, a wrinkle
deepening. I grew taller that day but still buckle when I see a weak
thing suffer. A papercut on my palm, a notch in the timeline of my life.

IN ORDER TO CRACK THE EGG WHILE PRESERVING THE YOLK

Write the punchline to the joke. In all seriousness:
today I learned: pigs recognize themselves in mirrors and
          a Great White named Mary Lee is lapping along the shores
               of New Jersey and
          you shouldn't wear black to a summertime wedding. Somehow
     in missing the social: in losing my dance card:
               in grasping a wider grip on my pores:
               I feel chlorophyll-full.

               I caught peril in a jar meant for pickling,
                    hung my two-step shoes on
     a long
               bronze hook. Today I learned: love is a sedimentary rock
with every wave washing over
               washing over   washing over   and lust is *so long!*—long
                    lost at sea.

     I want to stop writing about the ocean.
     I am rafted, mending the tool that might save me.

EXTINCTION

You said

you'd leave a missive   in brackish jade

but

the code

The electric-

effervescent glow could mean

vega, sirius, canopus

And this sand, it's glass

The paper   calcified, so gem-like   it shackles

us, something we once wanted

—& the message   wet

Every *m* smeared like   port   I'm looking for—

beyond the fog, more like sea smoke, starboard

For lunelight to take shape

Golden, round, rosy—it's shame

Tell the town

I sank

MINIMALISM

I am building a collapse.   Trying to explain what Mark Rothko   did
          to blurring.   I was told you had a cancerous mess in your chest so
I left town, looked for space.   You hate modern art, so I went
     there.   Tried to shake away this death, all the arranged glass
          that shattered then Robert Smithson reassembled, the shine of breath
                                        broken then refound in renewal.
& stillness borne by the Bechers—a strict and greyfull photograph,
          more ocean
                                than the ocean when the ocean wants to rest.
               As reliable as your window. This portrait, more honest now.
                    I want to fill this Donald Judd box with ancient
          items, brim it over   with the alive and dead, alive and dead,
          warmmelt of wisdom in postal paper, grass-of-Parnassus
     half-bloomed,
seconds extinguishing in snuff boxes.   This building
          hoisting
                              & holding scale & saturation up with
                    microscrews, & you,
     a figure in a grid of white paper glued to a hospital bed.
Nonetheless: you are historical. A round character in this story
          where everything else lies flat, academic, one-dimensional. An
                         action painting &   a fable. If disease
     is a one-hued Knoebel painting, it is another artistic movement,

chewing away at our century, elbowing its way through time.
Sol LeWitt knew lines & I cannot, not any longer. I know why
you walked away from the modern.   I begin to keen
curves & pause, the pulse of black light on black walls on the striped
black &
white of your shirt, the fading that falls between some color &
no color at all.

ODE TO MY LOVER'S BED

Plenty of coffee. A noose
for stale air. I wasn't, I admit,
generous or kind. I never
rewound the videocassettes,
didn't return them, instead
built a shelf for my
verdigris orchids. They
died, eventually, as all
breathing things do. How much
rain can I catch in a bucket?
What nugget could I find
at the bottom of a well? When
I am alone, the red memory
that makes me aware of my
breath—and thus, my death—

CENTO OF PAST LOVERS

Hold your hand up
like a mitten; I'll show you
where I lived in the state
of Michigan. Should I bite
you harder? Christine,
I wish you hadn't
lied to me. I don't think
I've ever seen you wear pants.
I'll buy the whiskey.
I imagined that by now
you would have dumped me
and started dating Colin.
I want to leave
New York. I don't think
it's the right time for a dog.
Of course I'd date you
even if you didn't have teeth.
I don't drink that much.
In my dream, we were riding
a rollercoaster into the state
of Maine. You're going
to get better. I once thought
I would like to marry you.

Do you think we should
move to California? It's only
a little blood. Why don't you
talk about your father more?
I wrote you a letter.
The tension between you
and your mother makes
me uncomfortable. You can't
always help me find a job. Your
calves are frameable. We can't
get a dog. I don't think I want
to be in any of your poems.
It feels weird to go out,
just the two of us, going
out, drinking? It feels
weird. Someday we will
attend a gala. Christine,
the teapot is boiling. When
my best friend told me
his mom had cancer, I didn't
flinch but I let him cry
on my shoulder. Read
Guy de Maupassant to me.
I wrote a song about you.
You overcooked the eggs.
I bought you that stupid
Japanese stuffed tooth
thing. God, you and your
obsession with juice.

Do you still love him?
Was I really sleepwalking?
In my dream, you were
blonde, had longer legs.
I don't have the patience
right now to listen to you
read poems. We could move
to Illinois, my parents are
in Illinois. You're terrible
with directions. You buy
too many dresses.
Isn't that skirt a little
short? I get it, you like dogs.
I'm taking the cat with me.
Try pork. I don't believe
in marriage. I won't always
be poor. I never told you this,
but my parents don't sleep
in the same bed. I drew the
state of New Jersey. You'll
know they're the right
mushrooms if they turn
blue when you pinch
them. I can't believe you
had me make dinner on my
own birthday. My dad snores.
You look at your phone
too much. Talk to me. Don't
talk to me. It doesn't cross

my mind to think about
you while I'm at work.
I don't appreciate your
desire to buy a home, even
if it is a long way's off.
Why don't you eat meat?
What if I wrap my fingers
around yours? Is that
too rough? Too soft? You
look like a kitten. Yes,
we can go sailing.
No, I don't really want to hike.
What feels right?
I don't think the solution
to the problem is to drink
more. Take the train to
St. James. I'm too stressed
for sex. I decided I can't
pick you up from the airport,
or—anywhere ever again.
I don't know how I feel.
I don't think I miss you.
I can't believe you told
Melissa we slept together.
I don't want you to call
me your partner. What
would you name the dog?
What if you slept
in a tent in the living room?

Try listening to Holst
while mapping the stars.
That's crazy, of course
I care about you. I wanted
to write, but I'm numb.
You're so fucking morbid.
I don't think the solution
to the problem is to adopt
a chinchilla. I made a film
for you. I'm moving.
I'm selfish. I can tell you
want to leave. I don't think
I can love anyone. Should
we be having more sex?
What if we learned to play
tennis? We could take LSD.
Call me your boyfriend.
Beige washes you out.
There's no way I have more
shoes than you. I can barely
pay for a MetroCard,
what makes you think
I could ever afford a dog?
I dreamt we were camping
on the prow of a ship.
Men have insecurity issues
too. I can tell you're
somewhere else. Your brain
is not like my brain.

I came home to your
messy house and I knew
this was over. Meet me
in the park after work.

SHAPES

—are relevant. As I was the almond-shaped, I wished

for a new sun. My professor moonlighted as a sex writer

and described her yoga

instructor—   as belly-front and kidney-shaped,

her toes bent backwards to her forehead.

This is a shape of fat, she did not say.

The O-shape your mouth makes when you yawn. When you cum.

With grass in my mouth   I measured yards by loopers, by inchworm,

—the shape

of nature. I lost the bet. I count mileage, gas-usage,

insurance and paychecks. The shape of the dollar sign, the hope

I fit the form to be good.

What's the shape for bad?

I shopped for a mold with gold edges, a gilded box to call

home. I notched the box until she bled.

I bled, too.

THE LETTING GO

I am writing because

I am in the forest. It is loud, muffling the white noise my heart locks up.

An animal who has found salt in the forest will return time and again to the spot.

Inebriate of air — am I

An animal. A wanting one. Of the senses, that commotion.

There are healthy ways to suffer, writes Lewis Hyde. But what if you suffer all the time? The clocks make you suffer, you are insufferably late, and once you arrive, nothing but cotton in your mouth? Nothing but calloused feet—you are used, often.

Inebriate of air — am I

Moving away from the crushed shell in me.

The dashes of highway, the highway that frames the forest. It used to be the other way around, a forest keeping a highway in, labyrinth of tree, but we keep building and building.

I am writing because

Julie says this is about beautiful girls. She means the word beautiful much more profoundly than it appears here. She really means it. Girls with symmetrical faces, the kind of girl who always eats for free, drinks for free, who gets away with dozens of mistakes, every day.

Julie: *There are a lot of beautiful girls who don't like alcohol. I wish I had a story about them—but in my truth, there are no beautiful girls who don't drink.*

The pressure, the self-edit. How will we find our way out of the forest?

Julie: *I am sure of only one thing—that realizing I was a girl who would become a woman came just before the drinking, and that without one I wouldn't have experienced the other.*

Julie says this is also about the fathers, we have to talk about the fathers. As much about the fathers as the mothers.

But then

What was invented. The memories I should be able to recall about my childhood, I have made them up. Drinking to be or feel more beautiful, then wanting to be *less*, again. To start somewhere and always end up in the same place. A hamster on a wheel. My memories sometimes a tourniquet around me, sometimes fireflies I am trying to catch, always two arm-lengths out of reach, always in the pitchblack.

**

The camera cuts

**

Another way to say this is: there is a history that belongs to me that I was not given. Instead, I was offered a mere reflection or distortion of assimilation. It is the white wash, the Xerox, the painted-over—how I must take and unravel it—that is how I will find this tale.

I measure every Grief I meet
With narrow, probing, eyes —

**

I was nearly a teenage, so many years blurred by, when I learned my parents had never been married, and later I would take pride in that, a little glass bottle, a fact unbreakable, out to sea. I did not have to explain myself to anyone, because I understood freedom differently. I understood loneliness differently, too.

**

The last time I visited my mother I told her I did not want to drink wine, did not think that at that moment it would cure the anxiety that swarms me like mosquitoes. The anxiety that creeps up and numbs you—it is so unsuspecting—and only later do you see you are uncontrollably scratching at yourself, medical-red, covered in hives.

My mother tells fifteen year old me that she needs to wear more makeup, be more assertive, stand up straight, asking *Are you on your period, you look a little bloated?*

Los Angeles has a reputation for its balmy weather, but the mornings are brisk. The wind comes off the ocean with intention and force, like an aggressive salesman.

I am learning how to look people in the eye.

June Jordan: *Poetry is a political act because it involves telling the truth.*

Whose truth, this time?

**

The camera cuts

**

My mother saying *This isn't hard alcohol, that makes it okay.* Retelling the story of my grandmother pouring Jack Daniels into cans of Pepsi to try and fool her children, but of course they knew. They knew as each batch of mashed potatoes Thanksgiving after Thanksgiving grew more and more buttery, until one year the bowl consisted of twelve sticks of butter and two potatoes, her hands shaking as she served us. This story told to me to be a lesson from my mother to herself, never meaning to instruct me: that what she drank, because it was expensive white wine, made the drinking okay, no matter how much, how many glasses. This is a parable about class, this is a story of being marginalized. Cut into.

No matter that she drank to kill an anxiety, to try and un-remember. Not forget, because forgetting happens by accident. This is active, and you need every artery, capillary, all the systems, musculoskeletal, digestive, endocrine, immune, respiratory—they must all cooperate.

My sentiments to share —

My grandmother drank because her husband carried on a fifteen-year affair. She drank more when my grandfather's mistress's son started dating her daughter, my aunt. On her deathbed they made amends, my aunt having married the man whose face, to my grandmother, read only of deceit, malintent, heartbreak. My grandmother died because she drank herself to death. A very drawn-out suicide. You cannot call it anything else.

Grant me, Oh Lord, a sunny mind —

My mother was and is a beautiful woman. A symmetrical face and full features, her figure lanky but spright, energetic and enthusiastic down to her fingerprints. Her only physical flaw I have noted: her nails. Thick, jagged, unappealing as cardboard hardened by mud, by a storm; she never took care of them or she took care of them too much when she was younger so that they gave up, grew hard with bitterness. Brittle.

As if her nails carried the burden of the past that she tried to un-remember. The man who raped her, her father who beat her, the things I don't even know about my father. I do not know what he did or didn't do to her. I have elected to not know this, and if I once knew it, to wash it away from me, as easy as picking off a scab. Almost— masochistically—enjoyable.

The Grieved — are many — I am told —

**

The men in my life who hurt her or hurt my grandmother directly or indirectly—directly or indirectly, I grieve.

**

These men, not my father.

**

My grandmother's nickname was Pinky. It did not carry any signifiers of ethnicity, even though my grandmother was half-Mexican, and, after the death of my grandfather, proud of it. My grandfather threw his Chinese name away long before I was born, and I never learned what it was.

**

Did my grandfather anoint Elizabeth, *daughter of Ernestina Nava*, Pinky? A book of erasure, rewriting of histories, assimilation and violence.

**

Once, when I was sixteen, my mother asked me at dinner if I wanted breast implants. "We can get them for you," she said. She did not see any malice in it. It was an unornamented ask, an ask similar to querying your guest: *would you like a glass of water?*

A draft in the kitchen. Los Angeles. Her many husbands.

No man I have loved has ever told me he has loved me back.

The confidence, the self editor, the forest.

An animal who has found salt in the forest will return time and again to the spot.

I am trying to tell you, and please believe me: *you can erase your own memory.* I am not advocating for it as I have been spending the last several years trying to get it back, the way you might dig through boxes and boxes of letters from past lovers, looking for the one clue that might solve the riddle of what destroyed the relationships, what went wrong.

An animal who has found salt in the forest will return time and again to the spot.

My memory like Dickinson's em dash, stopped and paused, put down, picked up again. An orange half peeled. One sock on, one off. Was this the way my brain was, from the beginning, or did I do this to myself?

Julie: *I will confess that there are times, while drinking, I've felt transcendent. Perhaps that sounds heavy-handed. Occasionally, let's say between drink three and before drink seven, depending on how much I've eaten and the rate at which I'm drinking, alcohol catapults me from my ever-watchful self, two steps outside of every experience (the note taker, an ex-boyfriend used to call me), to simply, completely,* there.

The camera cuts

**

My friends and I, we make jokes about the text message mistakes.
How I text Ethan while catsitting, say "This cat is so selfish" not notice
my mistake until much later, text again, I meant spoiled. *This cat is so
spoiled.* Send another text: Do I have early Alzheimer's? Laugh but I
feel like someone has pinched me, is really asking, in a stern medical
tone. I have to wonder.

When I go out to dinner with my mom, even if I intend to drink,
if I order any other beverage, any non-alcoholic beverage, her eyes
will widen. She jumps on me. Aren't you getting a drink, some wine.
Aren't you. *How many bullets bearest?*

Sometimes, I will do it. I will drink with her, not wanting to, because
I know, on some level, she can only be made more comfortable
this way. She, too, has that anxiety. Carrying the weight, the many
generations locked inside a locket.

You're right — "the way is narrow"

I read statistics, studies, one contradicting the other, about weather
patterns and wine drinkers, people who like whiskey and wake up
early, those who abstain and sleep in late. Drinkers with strong
hearts, drinkers with weak hearts. Drinkers hurt and drinkers in love.
Drinking to make a wish or to grieve the moon's departure when
dawn strikes.

A man once told me it wasn't anxiety, that it was depression. He recommended some tiny round pills you could dissolve at the bottom of your tongue. They'd break into tiny dots, fill the *sublingual papilla* with whiteness, with medication.

All the rooms are full.

**

The camera cuts

I am briefly outside of the forest. I am—

**

Myself, beachlit and alone. I escaped by driving for hours. The highway that frames the forest. Once I drove for two days and it took three for anyone to notice. I snuck out of my bedroom window on the first floor of our home, locked my door from the inside. My mother assumed I was just "going through a phase." I came home to my room untouched and unthought about. One envelope slipped under my door with money in it and a note from my father: *I hope you're okay. Are you?*

Was there a reason I should not be okay? What happened?

How dreary — to be — Somebody!

In a way, I was striked out. Blotted away. When my father died, my stepmother effectively erased me, because she hated me, hated my mother more, because, I was told, her own daughter had died, and her grief manifested itself in this way, a cloud of anger and frustration. She called newspapers and reporters to tell them I did not, do not, exist, took my name off of obituaries and claimed that my father's relationship with my mother was made-up, an early sign of the disease that would rot the muscle of his mind.

Remember, stuff the locket under the pillow: I had only recently learned that my parents had never married. The truth was a drop of water perpetually falling down a well. Who can catch the water? Who can stop it?

Julie: *A bit of advice for the daughter I hope to someday be good enough to have. Honey, tell them no. The best thing you can be is the wrong girl.*

Who was supposed to tell me you don't have to be the right girl for every man you meet?

My mother could not fight. Could not eat. Showered for hours because the locked bathroom was the most private place. She burned papers, paperwork, documents. She was too tired to fight. I was too high to care. Numb because and not because of a substance. Learning the act of un-remembering.

The lines of highway and lines of poem and Dickinson's em dash.

I know when the depression—I guess that's what we call it today, though I have always preferred to call it malaise—is setting in before the letting go. I'm usually alone and the sound of something in the distance becomes immediately pronounced, feels like it is coming out of me instead of it going into me, into each crooked hallway of my ear's canal. The sound starts to take on a shape, flattens my body. My skin then becomes very sensitive. There are rare times when, at this moment of the malaise, I can leave it. I can shut my eyes very tightly, and I can walk away. But usually I am locked in. My fingers go numb. That's how I really know. My fingers tingle, then they numb.

Despite all the burning, the heat, she drank. Despite the bonfires.

The camera cuts to a basement (but was it an attic? A den?)—

A scrap of paper I found, half-burnt, in my high school bedroom, my childhood home, before it was sold. Something I tried to write. *I come from a long line of failed marriages, deeply dysfunctional marriages, of alcoholics. Of female alcoholics.*

I make jokes about being adopted. Made them with my parents and my family frequently. They are uncomfortable, awkward, feel more like a plea, a wish, than an honest joke. And yet they say the best jokes are born from honesty. From the truth no one wants to talk about.

A line of women—the broken line—

This is assimilation: a story of men writing a history. This poem is an erasure.

**

Hyde: *In a blackout one is not passed out; he goes to parties, drives home, has conversations and so forth, but afterwards he has no memory of what he has done.*

Lewis Hyde writes about the he, but what about the she? The she blacking out to become less she. As if I could drink away this lineage. If I did not feel destined to fail. To die because you spend a lifetime trying to escape.

What I have to un-remember—to return to the line—to break it—

I have been trying to walk straight for too many years—*It sifts from Leaden Sieves*—I have been trying to escape—*It makes an even face*—I have created many reasons why I left the West—*It reaches to the fence—*

**

What I haven't spoken about is the mirror. Here goes. It feels like I'm plunging into deep water. I will take my clothes off, and I will see some version of myself in the mirror. I don't know anymore if it is actually what I look like or not. Things have become very blurry: there's the fat girl I see, there's the thin girl people tell me I am, there's the average sized, broad-shouldered woman I know I must be, given my measurements, my size, the way people talk about me.

**

It is true that sometimes I don't drink because my best friend is very skinny and never drinks and has lectured—not to me, but towards me—about the effects alcohol has on metabolic rates.

**

I was never told, as a child, *you are beauty. You are beautiful.* What was beauty but a cut-up piece of paper, and isn't it still? It look at the mirror and seek an inversion of the mirror. The mirror was once broken, and I repaired it with glue and the little pieces of my ancestors, whatever scraps I could find in the attic (but was it a basement, or a den?) of the house.

**

I run sometimes thinking about the calories in a glass of wine.

I spend the week waiting for Friday, when it feels "okay" to drink.

I am happy, I tell myself, to have a partner who doesn't really like to drink.

If I should disappoint the eyes / That hunted

**

I egged him on, not one night but several different nights, to drink with me. I said it would be fun, for the two of us, to go out and drink. I want so badly for him to treat me like a drunken hook-up, but I don't know why. I think there's some rush in it, but why am I scared of the quiet ordinary? I write now to remind myself: my partner is good to me. He is kind, generous, very loving. This is enough. This should be enough. Will you cement this idea with me, reader? Will you help me believe?

Necromancer, landlord, / Who are these below?

**

I write to Caitlin mostly because I want her to confirm that she's thought about driving a car into the woods and staying there. Forging her own, my own, kidnapping and escape. Could we actually get away with it? A more sane kind of suicide. Isn't it? The forest. *I can wade grief.*

I wrote once about how the only objects I remember from the room my grandfather died in are the small, tabletop fan, its clicking sound as it oscillated, one corner of the room to the next, one head of hair to rush in a flash, to the next. And the fly. A fly that buzzed hard against the small window that separated the room my grandfather was dying in from the room where nurses filled out paperwork, filled their cups with water from the water cooler, saw this damn thing every damn day.

**

Homesick for steadfast honey. I am and have been. If you keep leaving, you can displace home. There won't be memories of a childhood room, a door that creaked when the wind blew too hard. There is not much to the highway anymore.

To think just how the fire will burn—

✴✴

In longer stretches of time alone, I fill the void by writing letters to everyone in my orbit. I look for their words to consume me, distract me enough from my own need to reimagine the past or escape from it. To enter their world is to leave my own. To enter their orbit is to lose myself to the galaxy.

When I am alone, it is unacceptable to drink. When I am alone, I also think, plenty of people have martinis with their dinner. Plenty of people. They do it all the time.

✴✴

Thousands of miles away from California and in an impulsive fit I call my mother. She does not ask how I am, what I am doing, what am I wearing, is it cold, who I have seen, who I will see, if I will teach or not teach or who I will be with for lunch, dinner, breakfast, any of the forthcoming meals but she immediately launches into a series of complaints about her sisters. Her sisters who shame her for never holding a job, not for too long. Her sisters who never admit who they vote for in Presidential elections. Her sisters who want nothing more than for their daughters to marry up and have children, marry *wise* and marry *long*, even if none of these sisters have done it themselves. Not that that should matter, but divorce is a pattern humans tend to trace and follow, and this is okay, divorce is ok. Simply put, people change, just like the oceans heating, the waters rising. Urgency is relative.

We can't help us, who this family still aspires to be. Assimilation is a stern man's banking account. Even with the patriarch dead.

**

If I have not said *I do not blame her* then I will say it here: *I do not blame her*. I do not blame any of the woman in my family, or any of the women tied through them in the constellations—there are men who will take this blame when the galaxies turn over. For now, we are stuck in this one.

And this is a story of being overtaken by the forest. Those who taught the trees to maze are the ones who tear it down, exploit it.

So many bad men, lined up ready to enter the portal to the next galaxy.

**

I feel jealous, and feel bad for being jealous, when Julie tells me she made amends with her mother. The mother figure in her book, you see, was similar, but of course not the same, no one would want to say that, to her own mother. But her mother only saw herself. A kind of narcissism that runs like a river so deep it's wet to the center of the earth.

Julie's *book mother* was a functioning alcoholic. Was depressed, bad with men, picked the wrong ones. She had worn-and-prematurely ageing hands, from working as a housekeeper. I see slivers of my own mother here. This is what has brought Julie and me together. So many others, too—the women, the mothers, the lineage. The taking in and the letting go.

**

I drive away but I can no longer see the street signs, all the elms and non-native pines blurring my vision, emerald is what I can hold in me, all I have left—

**

But who owns this blame? If I cannot hold it, where does it go—does it fester like fresh dog bite? Or does it lay still, a robin's egg, luminous cyan given by a mother robin's blood, sleeping in a field of tall grasses?

**

I hold two boxes. In one, my resentment, anger, my inability to focus on the breathtaking way the Redwoods reach toward Orion. In another, the sadness for my mother, who cannot reveal her own story. It is littered with men who held knives at her, including her own father. It is marked by men cashing checks on assimilation.

That same box, songs my grandmother would sing in Spanish, the words I would pick up, repeat to myself before bed. The music is haunting.

**

The camera pans. The camera sweeps around the town square, panning to catch the eyes of all the women in this story. All of them at once, looking squarely at the camera, wiping one tear from each eye. No one waves.

**

After great pain, a formal feeling comes—

**

Of the *quartz contentment* Emily spoke of, I have been looking in the forest for every empty house. To find the others who may be seeking, in search of, have been lost in the forest, too. The little houses and their walls, black-and-burnt.

**

As Freezing persons, recollect the Snow —
First — Chill — then Stupor — then the letting go —

**

But what if, Emily, the letting go never goes?

Inebriate. Of air. Am I? And for whom?

PURLSPRUNG

Lanky
and elastic for each other.
The veil we lift, wink. The leaves
we lean to carry as a text
speaks to the lace.
We purlspring
these lines just for you, Reader.
Watcher. Stunner of our
intentions. How many ways
can we claim the word *pink*?

It's still sex even
with a chair on your head.
What a woman who loots
and hooks for the gaze, holds
it for another woman. Keeps
the gentleman with poor
eyesight and   primed cheeks
at bay.

Are you watching us undress
us thinking of undressing you?
Wax on, dear drifter. We are not against danger.
In fact

we are standing under its skirt,
unleashing its margin.

THERE WILL BE NO MORE DAUGHTERS

No nail to spark the fires, no waists
to nip in. There will not be cookery or
starguide, no petite or hardiness in lace,
hardly an elegance. No celebrities for
the TV. No dogearred books on floral
arrangement or patched socks, no darned
socks, no such darn thing. There will be
no more metal for the challenge.
There will be no more disaster of the street
signs. No treecrash or clunker, no perfume for
I Met You Then, of the hour, the whole hour,
needing more. There will not be timekeeping.
No luncheon on the knoll. No moors, definitely
not more than one. No Marnie. There will
be no more daughters. There will be no
more turquoise colonnade, no wallpaper worth
getting used to. No sticky toffee pudding.
Or plane ride of reward. Absolutely no thievery.
No sly cunning. There will be no wolves
and honeylapping. No desire. Not any
psychoanalytics. Nor the unstitching
or misreading of lips. There will not be
a breakfast. The oatmeal must stay cold.

No fixing of the bared and broken. No marking
the trails. There will be no more
horses. There will be no more daughters. Not
a single Daisy or a path, no guidance. No bluemoon,
bluemilk, or bluish undertones. No I'd Like
To Get To Know You Better. There aren't
any first dates here. There will be no more.
Not an Elissa. No plus or minus, no excess.
Not any malignant. No adherent or marrow
to remind anyone's alive. Not anyone at all,
no more alive than the stick-in-the-mud.
There won't be mud. There won't be a need.
There will be no more daughters. Never
a driver, no reaching, no end of the line—
no peach, no sweet—no taste of You and Me,
no plum—nothing neat. No sewing tidily.
No hem holding. No one getting handsy.
There won't be a truth or toothsome.
No, not an ounce or fling of it. Not a
pining for, never an I Would Do To You This
or That. There will never be pleat, no hat;
never long; not soft. Never Yes You Can,
Just This Once. There will not be anymore
skirmish, no getting high beneath the bleachers.
No sweaters. Wrecked and No I Liked
You Better When. No feeling up
and not a feeling at all. Not ever.

BIVALVE

But what of
      the molluscs?   Those
sweetmeats with sweethearted
      armor.   Whose possession
         of a wave
      curled inward.   Whose footless
            thrashing was
      the aftermath of
    clinical despair. On
the coordinates,
      I was entire
    and seabrittle, all
      greenglued on
the outside
    to hold history
        in.

ACKNOWLEDGMENTS

I am grateful to the editors of the publications in which some (often earlier versions) of these poems appeared: *Court Green*, *Sycamore Review*, *Narrative Magazine*, *The Literary Review*, *Pleiades*, *North American Review*, *Apogee*, and *Prelude*.

I'd like to thank D. A. Powell for selecting my poem "[This is where they planted the seeds]" for the Academy of American Poets University Prize, and later, to Mark Doty for including it in the *The Helen Burns Anthology: New Voices*; this award and this publication were my first of each. If I had not won that prize as an undergraduate, I don't know that I would have had the courage to write this book.

To my NYU teachers: Kimiko Hahn, Major Jackson, Sharon Olds; and classmates: Amanda Calderón, Gabe Habash, Dan Hamilton, Lizzie Harris, Sophie Herron, Mike Lala, Jen Levitt, Robin Coste Lewis, Virginia McClure, Amy Meng, Allyson Paty, Ben Purkert, Cat Richardson, Adam Soldofsky, Soren Stockman, Melissa Swantkowski, Ed Winstead, and Jenny Xie: thank you for your feedback, friendship, your time and readership, your encouragement and much-needed criticism. Thank you to Deborah Landau for running such a strong program with such a tightknit community, and for creating opportunities for students who need financial support.

All of my friends, writers and non-writers alike, who, every day, help me articulate what it means to be alive, who are family to me. I would do anything for you: Christopher Allen, Maia Fox Armaleo, Stephanie Bang, Rebecca Bechtel, Jeff Brenner, Emma Brenner-Malin, Sebastian Castillo, Olivia Ciummo, Michael Davidson, Emily Dunn, Amélie Garin-Davet,

Jon Golbe, Valentin Haddad, Steve Holmgren, Caitlin Hool, Hayat Hyatt, Caitlin Karosen, Alison Kobayashi, Katrina Mohn, Peter Romano, John Rutecki, SA Smythe, Joshua Solondz, Ethan Spaner, Aubrey Stallard, Sascha Stanton-Craven, and Tina Vargas.

Julie Buntin, your determination and creativity know no bounds. You are an inspiration to all writers. Thank you for being in my life and in this book. Thank you for always listening and for understanding. For knowing where I am coming from.

Morgan Parker—you have been the nucleus of my poetry world since we both moved back to California, and I feel connected to my writing and the writing of others in a completely transformative way thanks to you. I'm grateful to you for checking in on me, for pushing me to the finish line.

Carmen Giménez Smith, there are not enough words to express my gratitude to you for what you did: read 20 pages of my work and believed that it could become a book. Believed enough to award me the prize that would give me the time, money, space, and focus to let me make that book. I am so honored to be writing in the same universe as you.

I am immensely grateful to Madeleine Plonsker, for funding the residency and publishing prize at Lake Forest. The work I did at Lake Forest allowed this book found its real voice. There is no other prize like the Plonsker Prize, which places as much value on process as it does product.

To Joshua Corey and everyone at the English Department at Lake Forest College—my residency was warm, welcome, and happy because of you. Your kindness is unmatched.

Thanks to Jakob Vala for the beautiful book design. It is exactly how I always imagined it.

You can't read this because you're a dog, but Cooper, you're the best and give me so much joy when I need it (read: editing) and help me enjoy the outdoors more than I likely would without you. Thanks, pal. As I always say, I hope you live forever.

To my Mom, you're brave and strong and it's truly remarkable how much you've been able to do when so many have tried to keep you down. To my Father, I wish I could hand this book to you. Thanks to the rest of my family, especially those we grew up with who may not be blood-related but mean so much, just the same.

Rachel Zucker, for a very long time—over a decade, in fact—you have been my editor and my teacher, but you are also my family. I love you for reading so many drafts of my poems, bad ones and less-bad ones, for encouraging me from the first day of your undergraduate class to keep writing, for throwing poetry book after poetry book at me until I felt comfortable saying "I'm a poet." For showing me that this world of writing poetry was possible.

Without Colin Beckett, this book would not exist, as I probably would have found myself in a puddle of anxiety, unable to go on. Dear Colin, your love, editorial guidance, constant support, humor, intelligence, and all-around brilliance helps me keep going every day, in writing and in all other movements of life.

Thanks also to everyone who read this book. I'm honored you gave me your time.

NOTES

"I was a painter once" quotes Anne Sexton's poem "The Truth the Dead Know" and Frank O'Hara's poem "Nocturne."

"The Letting Go" includes quotations from J. E. Buntin's essay "Under the Table," originally published in *The Rumpus* (2013); Lewis Hyde's essay "Alcohol & Poetry: John Berryman and the Booze Talking," first published in *American Poetry Review* (October 1975); as well as various poems by Emily Dickinson.

CHRISTINE LARUSSO holds a BA from Fordham University (Lincoln Center) and an MFA in Creative Writing from New York University. Her poetry has appeared in *The Literary Review, Pleiades, Women's Studies Quarterly, Sycamore Review, Prelude, Court Green, Narrative,* and elsewhere. She is the 2017 winner of the Madeleine P. Plonsker Emerging Writer's Residency Prize, and has been named a finalist for both the Orlando Poetry Prize and the James Hearst Poetry Prize. Her poem, "Lunar Understanding," was nominated for a Pushcart. She is a Producer for Rachel Zucker's podcast, *Commonplace.* She is from Los Angeles, and currently lives there—after over a decade in Brooklyn—with her partner, critic/editor Colin Beckett and their dog.

The Madeleine P. Plonsker
Emerging Writer's Residency Prize

LAKEFOREST.EDU/PLONSKER

Yearly Deadline: March 1